THE REAL
GHOSTBUSTERS™

SLIMER COME HOME

When Slimer eats one cake too many,
such is his shame that he leaves his
Ghostbuster companions and turns, in his
loneliness, to some new – and dangerous
– friends . . .

Ghostbusters are here to save the world!

The third title in the Real Ghostbuster™
Series

Egon's Laboratory

THE REAL GHOSTBUSTERS™

SLIMER COME HOME

novelisation by
Kenneth Harper

Illustrated by Jon Miller

KNIGHT BOOKS
Hodder and Stoughton

First published in Great Britain by Knight Books 1988

Printed and bound in Great Britain for Hodder and Stoughton Paperbacks, a division of Hodder and Stoughton Limited, Mill Road, Dunton Green, Sevenoaks, Kent TN13 2YA (Editorial Office: 47 Bedford Square, London WC1B 3DP) by Cox and Wyman Limited, Reading, Berks. Photoset by Rowland Phototypesetting Limited, Bury St Edmunds, Suffolk.

British Library C.I.P.

Harper, Kenneth, *1940–*
  Slimer Come home.
  Rn: Keith Miles
  I. Title   II. Miller,
  Jon *1947–*
  823′.914[J]

ISBN 0-340-42134-7

1

Lonesome Winston

Night drew a blanket of darkness over New York City. At the old fire station which acted as Ghostbuster Headquarters, everything was peaceful. After a long day, they were all relaxing in the lounge area on the first floor. It was a large, cluttered, comfy place on which they had stamped their character.

There was furniture, a television, sound equipment, a computer, plenty of books and dozens of games. The atmosphere was pleasant and they loved being in it. They had turned the room into something very special.

A real home.

Egon Spengler was seated at the table, poring over the plans for his latest invention. Tall, thin and with a quiff of fair hair, Egon was a serious and rather solemn young man. His eyes glistened behind his spectacles. He was in love with science.

Egon had designed the laboratory up on the top floor and all the equipment that the Ghostbusters used. But

5

he was a perfectionist and so he was never satisfied. As soon as one of his inventions was in use, he wanted to improve it or adapt it.

'Science is the art of perfection,' he always said.

And he was determined to prove it.

Ray Stantz was lying on the sofa and reading a book about poltergeists. Something caught his eye and he murmured to himself.

'Hey! That's interesting!'

An active, affable, chunky man, Ray was completely involved in his work as a Ghostbuster. Nobody knew as much about Weird Things and their past as Ray. He was a walking encyclopedia of bizarre facts.

Ray was a true scientist who would confront the unknown without a tremor in the name of research. While others might be frightened by supernatural happenings, he was *fascinated*. Ray had another role as well. He was the mechanic on the team. His skilful hands built all the equipment that Egon designed.

'That's amazing!' he muttered, studying his book.

Dr Peter Venkman was sprawled in a chair as he watched a cartoon series on television. A tall, dark-haired, alert character, Peter had helped to found the Ghostbusters and organise their work. He was a sharp-witted, fast-talking character who was something of a showman. Though he never looked for trouble, he would always fight his way out if he was cornered.

Peter laughed at the cartoon and reached out to take a handful of popcorn from the large bag beside him. Eating any food in the lounge was difficult.

There was always a threat.

Slimer.

His eyes never left the bag of popcorn.

Slimer was a green ghostie who had become the mascot of the Ghostbusters. He was their first-ever captive, and he had slimed Peter on that occasion. A large, shapeless blob of ectoplasm, he had an insatiable appetite. As soon as he saw food, he wanted it.

'Guzz-guzz-guzz-guzz!'

'*No*, Slimer!' warned Peter.

'Weeeeee!' whimpered the ghost.

'They're *mine*.'

Slimer hovered in mid-air above the popcorn, eyes fixed on it.

It looked crisp and sweet and delicious.

Winston Zeddmore flicked idly through a magazine. He was the only one of the Ghostbusters without a scientific training. But he had many sterling qualities. Tough, courageous and intensely practical, Winston was a vital member of the team. He was also the warmest and friendliest of them.

Putting his magazine aside, he turned to Ray Stantz.

'Say, how about a game of cards?'

'No, thanks,' replied Ray.

Winston shrugged and looked across at Egon instead.

'Fancy a game of chess?'

'No, thanks,' said Egon.

Winston was disappointed. He called over to Peter.

'What say we throw a little dice, man?'

'Forget it.'

'You can go first.'

'Count me out,' said Peter.

Winston was hurt. All three of his colleagues were ignoring him. It was most unusual and he could not understand it. He stood up in the centre of the room.

'What's the matter with you guys?' he demanded.

'Nothing,' said Ray.

'Nothing whatsoever,' added Egon.

'Nothing whatsoever in any shape or form,' agreed Peter.

'So why are you freezing me out?'

'We're not,' they said in unison.

Then they carried on with what they were doing.

Winston grinned as a wicked idea came into his head.

'Hey, Slimer, how about a popcorn-eating contest!'

Slimer did somersaults of pure joy.

'Guzz-guzz-guzz!'

He swooped on the popcorn but Peter batted him away.

'Don't you *dare*, Slimer!' he shouted.

'Weeeeee!' protested the ghost.

Slimer flew up to the ceiling and snuffled quietly.

'It's all your fault, Winston,' said Peter. 'Look at the state you've gotten him into now. Why d'ya suggest a fool thing like a popcorn-eating contest?'

Slimer swooped back down hopefully.

'Guzz-guzz-guzz!'

'That wasn't an invitation!' yelled Peter, pushing him away.

9

'Weeeeee!'

Slimer retreated in bruised silence.

'See what you did, Winston?' said Peter.

'Slimer's the only guy around here who'll listen to me.'

Winston walked across to the stairs with dignity.

'I'm gonna talk to Janine. *She'll* show an interest.'

He went quickly down the stairs, nursing his hurt feelings. As soon as he had gone, the other three exchanged a conspiratorial grin. They were working to a deliberate plan.

'Think he suspects?' said Ray.

'Not a chance,' replied Peter.

'Now it's up to Janine,' added Egon.

The reception area was on the ground floor of the building. It had desks, telephones, lamps, screens and a bank of filing cabinets. It was the private domain of Janine Melnitz, the tireless secretary to the Ghostbusters. Janine was a tall, attractive, rather scatty-looking young woman with glasses on the end of her nose and a world-weary air. Nothing could shake her. She was highly efficient. Though she had a soft spot for Egon, she kept her feelings hidden and she would take the Ghostbusters to task if she thought they deserved it. Which they often did.

Janine was a very independent and outspoken girl.

Even at that late hour, she was working. As Winston came into the room, she was peering into the open drawer of a filing cabinet. Something was intriguing her.

'Hi, Janine!' called Winston.

'Oh!'

She turned in surprise and slammed the drawer shut.

'CLANG!'

'Why did you creep up on me like that?' she demanded.

'I was only being friendly.'

'You made me jump out of my skin,' she scolded. 'Back off.'

'I only wanted a chat.'

'I'm too busy, Winston.'

'Just like everyone else!' he said ruefully.

'I'm sorry but you'll have to excuse me.'

'Where are you going?'

'I have to discuss something with the others.'

'What about *me*?' he asked.

'This doesn't concern you.'

Janine went striding towards the staircase. Winston sighed then walked after her. When he got back upstairs, there was further upset for him. Janine was whispering to the others.

'Did you get what I asked, Ray?' she said.

'Sure, sure.'

'What about you, Egon? Did you buy what I told you?'

'Yeah, Janine.'

'Peter?' she whispered. 'Did you collect those whatnots?'

'Of course.'

'Then it's all under control, guys.'

'Check!' they chorused.

Winston ambled over to them.

'Say, is this a private party or can anyone join in?'

They all began to smirk and snigger.

'What's going on here?' howled Winston.

'Nothing,' said Ray.

'Nothing whatsoever,' added Egon.

'Nothing whatsoever in any shape or form,' agreed Peter.

Janine put it even more bluntly.

'Nothing whatsoever in any shape or form that need bother you. This is *our* business, Winston. Give us a little privacy.'

'Oh . . . right.'

Winston looked sadly around then tramped off upstairs.

The four of them giggled among themselves.

The dormitory was on the top floor of the building. It had four beds and an array of chairs, tables, wardrobes, books, paintings and hanging plants. Winston came in and sat down on the edge of his bed, trying to work out what he had done wrong. It was puzzling.

In the floor nearby was a circular hole where the firemen's pole ran down to the ground floor. Something zipped up through the gap and hovered in front of him.

It was Slimer.

'Glug-glug-glug.'

'I got one friend at least,' he said gratefully.

'Glug-glug-glug.'

'What's happened to the guys?' he asked. 'They've

13

been funny with me all day. I don't like it. Ever get the feeling you're being shut out, Slimer?'

'Glug-glug-glug.'

Slimer nodded vigorously and a few blobs of ecto-plasm flew off. Muffled laughter came from the room below. He glanced down through the hole.

'*They're* having fun,' moaned Winston.

'Glug-glug-glug.'

'But what about *me*, Slimer?'

The ghost tried to console him with soothing noises.

'Coo-coo-coo-coo!'

'Thanks,' said Winston. 'You're a real pal.'

More laughter drifted up through the opening in the floor.

Winston felt lonely and shut out.

The other Ghostbusters were his closest friends.

What *was* going on?

2

Shadowing Shadows

There was something ominous about the night. As the man and the woman walked home through the darkness, they quickened their footsteps. It was one of the rougher neighbourhoods in New York and they sensed trouble. Turning a corner, they hurried on.

Streetlights cast pale yellow circles on the sidewalks. A few cars cruised slowly by, their headlights scissoring a way through the gloom. The sky was a heavy black coverlet. Light spilled out from behind a few of the curtained windows.

The man and the woman felt more and more uneasy.

'What is it?' she asked.

'Nothing,' he said.

'Are we being *followed*, dear?'

'Keep walking.'

The streetlight ahead of them flickered and went out.

'What happened?' she asked in mild alarm.

'I guess the bulb went,' he said.

'It's much darker now.'

'Let's move it.'

But they did not get very far. As they tried to lengthen their stride, something came out to block their way with a hideous clatter. The noise was deafening.

'Crash! Bang! Miaouw!'

A dustbin rolled out into their path. The cat, which had been sitting on the lid, went screeching off down the street like a ball of fur. It was as terrified as they now were. Stepping around the bin, they continued on their way.

The woman gripped the man's arm more tightly.

'I'm scared,' she admitted.

'We'll be okay,' he said, trying to reassure her.

'I think there's somebody behind us.'

'There isn't, I tell you.'

'No? You listen.'

The man did and he gulped loudly. Footsteps were indeed stalking them. Too frightened to look back, they put on extra speed and turned around the first corner to shake off their pursuer.

But the footsteps stayed right behind them.

'What does he want?' she said nervously.

'Not far to go now.'

'Why doesn't he leave us alone?'

'Try to ignore him.'

It was impossible to do that. The footsteps got louder and closer all the time. As they passed another street-light, their own shadows strode out in front of them.

Then they saw something which threw them into a panic.

There were only two of them.

But there were three shadows.

'Look!' she gasped, pointing.

'It's getting bigger and bigger!' he exclaimed.

'Who is it?'

'Quick – down here!' he advised.

Steering her around another corner, he tried and failed again to lose whoever was trailing them. This time it was worse. The street was a dead end. There was no way out.

The third shadow was now enormous, engulfing them both.

Jaws slack and eyes like poached eggs, they swung around to confront their tormentor. The man spoke in a trembling voice.

'What do you *want*?'

But there was nobody there.

The shadow ended at the feet but there was no human being to cast it. They were baffled. They were also very relieved.

'Thank goodness!' she said.

'We must've imagined those footsteps,' he decided.

'But where did the shadow come from?'

'A trick of the light.'

'Yet it's so big.'

They turned around to see the shadow which now covered half the wall in front of them. As they watched, its eyes started to glow and a long, snouty nose

appeared. In a flash, the shadow turned into a menacing giant with a pig-like face.

It swooped on them with relish.

'Boo!'

Hysterical with fear, they took to their heels.

'Arghhhhhhhhhh!'

The shadow was alive.

The Ghostbusters were still relaxing in their headquarters. Ray, Egon and Peter were having a whispered chat in the lounge as if discussing a secret plan. Winston was up in the dormitory with Slimer. He was still feeling that he had been cold-shouldered by the other Ghostbusters and it wounded him. He was one of the team.

Why should they treat him like an outsider?

Winston's thoughts were rudely interrupted.

BRRING-BRRING!

The alarm bell galvanised him into action.

BRRING-BRRING! BRRING-BRRING!

He went straight to the pole and slid down it. Ray, Egon and Peter did exactly the same thing. All four ended up in the reception area in front of the desk.

Janine waved a slip of paper at them. It contained the details of the emergency call which she had just taken. Peter collected the memo from her.

'Same thing?' he asked.

'Yeah,' she said.

'Same place?'

'Yeah?'

'Same problem?'

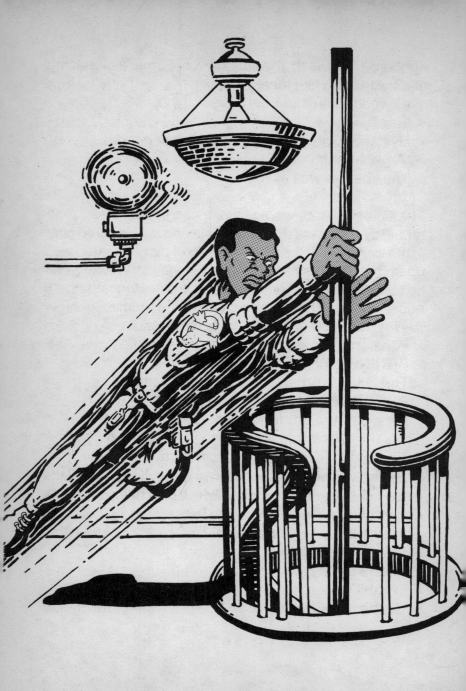

'Yeah.'

'Okay, Ghostbusters!' ordered Peter. 'Let's hit the road!'

Egon, Ray and Winston ran off to Ecto-I. Peter lingered so that he could have a quiet word with Janine.

'This gives you the perfect chance,' he told her.

'I know.'

'We'll keep him out as long as we can.'

'Leave the rest to me.'

Ray beeped the horn on Ecto-I. He was anxious to be off.

'See you later!' called Peter, running to the car.

'Good hunting, guys!' shouted Janine.

She waited until the car engine roared and the vehicle shot out through the open doors. Then she got up from her desk and came to the middle of the room. She rubbed her hands purposefully together.

The Ghostbusters had left her alone at last.

Janine was grateful.

There was a lot to do.

Ecto-I sped through the streets of New York with its siren wailing and its light bar flashing. It had started life as an ambulance but it had been adapted to their own special needs. But like an ambulance, it spent all its time dashing to a crisis.

Ray Stantz was at the wheel with Peter beside him. Egon and Winston were in the rear of the vehicle. They headed for the rough neighbourhood where the couple had been shadowed by the shadow. It was not the first time they had been there.

'Three nights in a row!' said Ray.

'It has to be the same group,' decided Peter. He lowered his voice to whisper to Ray. 'At least it gives us an excuse to keep you-know-who out of the station until you-know-what is ready.'

'What's that?' asked Winston.

'Nothing,' said Peter.

'Something funny's going on around here,' insisted Winston.

'Yeah,' said Egon. 'We gotta poltergeist on the loose.'

'I was reading a book about poltergeists,' said Ray with interest. 'Poltergeist means noisy ghost. They throw things about or ring bells or even start fires. Serious physical injury is rare although great force is displayed at times.'

'That's right,' agreed Egon.

'I don't get it,' said Winston. 'Why would poltergeists go after random targets in this neighbourhood? I thought they usually stayed in one place?'

'They do,' said Peter.

'Don't they get weaker the further they go?' asked Winston.

'Usually, yes,' explained Egon. 'But this case is very strange indeed. They shouldn't have the energy for roving attacks. Unless they have a source.'

He was studying the PKE meter which he held in his hand. It measured the amount of Psycho-Kinetic Energy left behind or generated by ghosts. Designed by Egon

himself, the meter was a highly sensitive instrument. It had tiny wings on the top. The left one began to flash a warning.

'Left!' yelled Egon.

Ray Stantz pulled hard on the steering wheel.

'Screeeeeeeeeeech!'

Ecto-I skidded around the corner on two wheels, hit a kerb then bounced back on to the road. Peter and Winston were hurled against the side of the vehicle.

'Whoa!'

'Aaaaaaak!'

Egon was hypnotised by the meter. He did not see the way in which his colleagues had been thrown about.

Peter tried to be diplomatic about it.

'Say, ah, Egon,' he began, 'you think we could have a little more warning next time? Not to get personal, of course, but –'

'Right!' ordered Egon.

Ecto-I went around another hairpin bend.

'Scruuuuuuuuuuunch!'

Peter and Winston were hurled against the other side now.

'Hey!'

'Hold on there!'

'Are you trying to kill us, Egon?'

'Slow down!'

Peter and Winston picked themselves up from the floor and dusted themselves off. It was proving to be a rocky journey.

Egon looked up from his PKE meter.

'Now – what did you say, Peter?'

'I can't remember,' said Peter, still dazed.

'But it sounded important.'

'I said . . .' Peter shrugged. 'Oh, never mind.'

Ecto-I came to a teeth-rattling halt.

'Guddunk!'

The Ghostbusters got out at once. Egon was still staring at his meter as it flashed wildly. The others looked around.

'Okay,' said Winston. 'Where to now?'

'Your guess is as good as mine,' admitted Peter.

'They must be here *somewhere*,' argued Ray.

They were then given a very obvious clue.

'Eeeeeeeeeeeek!'

A horde of screaming people came running around a corner and charged past them. Their arms were high in the air and their hair was standing on end. They had had a terrible fright.

Ray, Winston and Peter knew where the trouble was.

'Left!' they shouted in unison.

They set off in that direction with their Proton Guns at the ready. Egon, meanwhile, studied his PKE meter. He raised a long finger and pointed over to the left.

'It's coming from there.' He realised he was alone. 'Oh. They must tell me how they do that some time.'

Egon caught them up. All four strode bravely on.

Strange noises and a bright, unnatural light were coming from an alley up ahead. The Ghostbusters marched on and turned into the alley. They halted and stared in horror.

'Look at that!' said Peter.

'It's like nothing we've ever seen before,' added Winston.

'This could be a scientific breakthrough,' said Ray.

'We're in serious trouble here,' warned Egon.

They were faced by a huge, whirling tornado.

It was coming towards them.

3

Rubbishing Ghosts

The tornado gathered strength with each second. It was dark, devilish and deafening. At its heart were some strange wraith-like creatures. Pale and almost transparent, they were dancing happily and shouting with glee.

'Whoooooooooooooooo!'

'Yaaaaaaaaaaaaaaaa!'

'Zeeeeeeeeeeeeeee!'

The Ghostbusters held their Proton Guns up.

'What a fantastic sight!' said Ray, open-mouthed in wonder.

'I prefer watching TV,' said Peter with alarm.

'Whoever heard of a tornado in New York?' said Winston.

'Now, remember,' urged Egon, trying to bolster their morale. 'Poltergeists can't actually hurt you.'

The ghosts seemed to take this as a challenge.

With sudden venom, the tornado swooped down and

gathered up all the trash cans in the alley. They whirled in the air and then one of the wraiths started to pile them on top of each other. He soon had a pile of metal bins as high as the rooftops.

'Poltergeists can't hurt us,' repeated Egon, getting worried. 'But trash cans sure can!'

'They're going to fall!' warned Ray.

'Hold your ground!' commanded Peter.

'But they'll hit us,' argued Winston.

'No,' retorted Peter. 'We blast 'em!'

The trash cans fell through space towards them.

Synchronising their particle throwers, they fired.

'KAPOUW!!!'

The metal bins disintegrated in the blast but the garbage kept on coming. The Ghostbusters were covered by a wave of egg shells, empty tins, waste paper, food scraps and other refuse.

'Urgh!' complained Winston.

'All over me!' protested Egon.

'This is your fault, Peter,' accused Ray.

'Okay, okay,' said Peter defensively. 'I saw three Clint Eastwood movies last night and I got carried away. Sue me.'

They started to wipe off the worst of the garbage.

But the ghosts had not finished with them yet.

Before they could escape, they saw the tornado circling them at speed. They were completely trapped.

'Uh, oh!' said Ray. 'It's showtime, folks.'

'I don't like this!' admitted Winston.

'Scientifically, it's quite intriguing,' said Egon.

29

'Recharge your guns, guys,' ordered Peter.

They switched on their Proton Guns and the power surged.

'Ready!' said Ray.

'Ready!' said Peter.

'Ready!' said Egon.

'Ready!' said Winston.

The bright light that was given off by the ghosts threw shadows on to the wall. The Ghostbusters saw their own four shadows being joined by a fifth. It was bigger than all the others put together and it suddenly had a wicked, grinning, pig-like face.

'Trouble,' noted Ray.

'Big trouble,' added Winston.

'Very big trouble,' conceded Egon.

'Very, very, very, *very* big trouble,' exclaimed Peter.

Their predictions came true at once.

The tornado engulfed them and they were lifted high into the air. Whirling around helplessly in space, they had no chance to use their guns. They went faster and faster.

'Put me down!' howled Ray.

'I haven't got a flying licence!' yelled Peter.

'I'm getting dizzy up here!' shouted Winston.

'Poltergeists are not supposed to *do* this kind of thing!' cried Egon, sticking to the scientific niceties.

Conducted by the shadow-monster on the wall, the ghosts were zipping around in an ever-increasing spiral and laughing maniacally. The Ghostbusters were

whisked around as if caught in some vast mixing machine.

The shadow-monster grinned evilly, pulled his black cloak around him and gave a loud hiss.

'Enough!'

Obeying his command at once, the ghosts streamed off towards an open manhole cover and vanished into the sewers.

Peter Venkman watched them go.

'Wait a minute,' he recalled. 'Didn't I see this in the Wizard of Oz?'

The shadow-monster raised his top hat in farewell then he disappeared into the sewers as well. The manhole cover clanged behind him. The ghosts had all fled the scene.

There was nothing to keep the Ghostbusters aloft.

They fell to the ground with a resounding thud.

'Aouw!'

'Errrrg!'

'Yiiiii!'

'Ooooooo!'

They were sitting amid mounds of smelly garbage.

'Talk about things that go bump in the night!' said Peter.

'I never want to ride a tornado again,' asserted Ray.

'This may take a little longer than we thought,' said Egon.

Winston removed a banana skin from his head.

'Well, guys,' he suggested. 'Look on the bright side.'

'The *bright* side!' they chorused.

'Yeah – it couldn't possibly get any worse.'

But it could. Much worse.

'SHAZAM!'

Forked lightning split the sky and the rain came at once. Torrents fell and they were soon embroiled in a sticky morass of rubbish. It was like being caught in a swamp.

Peter turned vengefully towards Winston.

'What was that you said?'

Ecto-I cruised slowly through the glistening streets. The heavy rain continued and the windscreen wipers flashed to and fro. Wet, weary and demoralised, the Ghostbusters sat in the vehicle with towels around their necks. They were a sullen bunch.

It was not often that they failed so abysmally.

Winston reflected on what had happened. The night had been a disaster for them but there was one consolation. When they had raced off in answer to the emergency call, he had been one of the team. They had accepted him. Now that the crisis was over, however, he felt like an outsider again.

The others were not talking to him.

Something else puzzled him. He looked out.

'We taking the long way home?' he asked.

'I'm the driver,' grunted Ray.

'Then why're we going so slow?'

'What's there to hurry about?' said Peter.

'We need to get back and clean up.'

'I like being dirty,' added Peter.

'There's no rush,' agreed Egon.

'I can't go any faster in this rain,' said Ray.

Winston folded his arms and turned away from them.

'Okay,' he said with resignation. 'Please youselves.'

In the front of the car, Ray winked across at Peter.

'Say,' he whispered, 'you think Janine's got everything set up by now?'

'I hope so,' hissed Peter.

'This'll really make his night!' said Ray.

They chuckled quietly.

Winston felt more isolated than ever.

They drove back to the fire station at a leisurely pace. The doors opened and Ecto-I rolled into its parking place, rain dripping from its gleaming bodywork. There was a last flash of lightning visible then the garage doors slammed shut.

The sodden Ghostbusters got slowly out of the car.

Winston led the way into the reception area.

It was dark, deserted and rather unwelcoming.

'Janine!' he called. 'Slimer!'

Dead silence. The place was as quiet and empty as a grave.

'Hey, where is everybody!' yelled Winston.

'WHAM!'

The lights snapped on and the place was bathed in light. Balloons, streamers and decorations were everywhere. The whole room was festooned. There was a warm, festive atmosphere.

Ray, Egon and Peter sang in unison.

'Surprise! Surprise!'

'What?' gasped Winston.

'Happy Birthday!'

'Oh,' said Winston, grinning. 'I'd forgotten.'

'We hadn't!' said Peter.

Janine and Slimer now came out of their hiding places behind the desk. Both were wearing and carrying cone-shaped party hats. Slimer zipped across to put a hat on Winston's head.

'Happy birthday!' congratulated Janine.

'I . . . I don't believe it,' said Winston, overwhelmed.

Janine handed party hats to the other Ghostbusters and they put them on. They all slapped Winston on the back.

'Well done, pal!'

'Sorry we had to freeze you out.'

'We didn't want to let you in on the secret.'

'And I thought I'd done something wrong!' said Winston.

'We kidded you along,' explained Peter.

'Yeah,' said Ray. 'And we kept you out of the office as long as we could so that Janine could put up the decorations.'

'No wonder you were driving so slow,' noted Winston.

'All part of the plan,' said Egon.

'It took a lot of organising,' added Janine.

'I can see that,' said Winston, looking around. 'Boy, you've really worked hard here. And all for *me*!'

'Of course,' said Peter.

'Why not?' asked Egon.

'You're one of us, pal!' affirmed Ray.

'Glug-glug-glug!' said Slimer excitedly.

Winston was absolutely delighted. He was no outsider now. He was among some very good and thoughtful friends.

'This is just terrific, guys!' he said.

'There's more to come,' promised Janine.

'Is there?'

She went to the back of the room and pushed out a trolley. Standing on the top of it was an enormous, three-tiered birthday cake. It was piped with blue and white icing.

'I don't believe it!' said Winston gaping.

'Blueberry fudgecake,' announced Janine. 'Your favourite.'

'All yours, Winston,' said Peter.

'Save a piece for us,' said Ray.

'I just want you to know,' said Egon with great seriousness, 'that I'm having a wonderful time.'

'We're *all* having a wonderful time,' said Janine. 'That's what parties are for, aren't they?'

Winston was staring at the cake in awe.

But so was somebody else.

Slimer.

His mouth slavered and his lips quivered.

Every ectoplasmic inch of him wanted that cake.

Slimer's eyes widened to the size of dinner plates.

Winston was so overcome that he had difficulty speaking.

'This is . . . wonderful,' he began. 'I . . . I really don't

know what to say . . . except that . . . this is the happiest day of my . . .'

He got no further.

The pressure on Slimer was too strong. He cracked.

Flashing across the room, he kept his mouth wide open.

'ZOOOOOOOOOOM!'

The whole cake vanished in one great gulp.

4

Oh, Slimer!

There was a stunned silence that lasted for almost a minute. They could hardly believe it. The trolley was now completely bare. In one massive, greedy, snake-like bite, Slimer had gobbled up a three-tiered birthday cake and all its decorations.

Anger and consternation erupted.

'No, Slimer!'

'Don't you dare!'

'Stop it!'

'That's Winston's cake!'

'Leave it alone!'

But the cries were too late. He was already munching.

'Chomp-chomp-chomp!'

Janine stalked across to confront the ghost.

'Slimer!' she scolded. 'How *could* you?'

'Gurrrrr.'

Slimer looked sheepish. He felt very guilty about what he had done. But he could not help it. Where food was

concerned, he had no self-control. The birthday cake had been too big a temptation. He simply had to have it.

'Glug-glug-glug,' he said apologetically.

'I'm ashamed of you!' chided Janine.

'Gurrrrr.'

Still munching, he retreated guiltily to a corner.

Ray put a consoling hand on Winston's shoulder.

'Tough luck, old buddy!'

'Yeah,' agreed Egon. 'Malignant misfortune.'

'It's okay,' said Winston, trying to hide his bitter disappointment. 'I'm on a diet, anyway.'

'You are now,' Egon pointed out.

'The whole surprise has been ruined,' moaned Ray.

'Forget it,' said Winston. 'I told you. It's okay.'

Peter Venkman took over with authority.

'Hang on a second,' he insisted. 'It's *not* okay!'

He strode across to Slimer who was hovering in his corner.

'We planned this party all week, Slimer.'

'Gurrrr.'

'It means a lot – to us and to Winston. But you have to go and mess it up!'

Slimer looked shamefaced. He took off his hat.

'Gurrr,' he whimpered, offering the hat to Peter.

With a burst of anger, Peter knocked it out of his hand.

'That's not going to make up for it!'

Egon moved in to add a conciliatory word.

'Let it go, Peter,' he suggested. 'What's done is done.'

'Yeah,' said Ray. 'No good crying over spilled milk – or over gobbled cake!'

'It's my party, after all,' said Winston half-heartedly. 'Slimer just couldn't help himself.'

Peter's ire was only increased by the remark.

'Are you kidding?' he demanded. 'He helps himself to everything that isn't nailed down or on fire! But what use is he? Huh? Tell me that!'

He rounded on Slimer again and pointed a finger at him.

'The first time I saw you, you slimed me!' he yelled.

'Weeeee,' squealed Slimer.

'You've been nothing but trouble ever since,' continued Peter harshly. 'So do us all a favour – cut it out, okay?'

Slimer hung his head in disgrace and sobbed.

'We've had just about enough of you!' added Peter.

The ghost whimpered again then drifted up to the ceiling. After a last glance back at them, he floated up through the hole around the fire-pole. If he had had a tail, it would have been between his legs.

Peter's face was stern as he watched Slimer go.

The others were more sympathetic to their pet ghost.

'You were awfully hard on him, Peter,' said Ray.

'He deserved it.'

'The punishment should fit the crime,' suggested Egon.

'In that case, Winston should eat *him*,' retorted Peter.

'Oh, I don't blame Slimer,' said Winston. 'It wasn't really his fault. He's not made the way we are.'

'Someone had to call him to order,' said Peter.

'Maybe,' agreed Ray. 'But I think you hurt his feelings.'

Peter shuffled his feet then shrugged his shoulders.

'Well,' he said grudgingly. 'He has to learn. Besides, ghosts don't have feelings.'

'Slimer does,' answered Ray. 'I think so, anyway.'

The party was over. They all heaved a deep sigh.

'Time to get some shut-eye,' suggested Peter.

'Good idea,' said Egon. 'I'm exhausted.'

'I'll sleep till doomsday,' said the yawning Winston.

After a flurry of farewells, the three of them tramped wearily upstairs. Ray was about to follow them when Janine spoke.

'Are you serious about what you just said?'

'Slimer? Having feelings?'

'It's impossible.'

'Is it, Janine?'

'Yes,' she argued. 'I mean, a ghost is a ghost. They just don't have emotions like us.'

Ray looked up in the direction that Slimer took.

'No?' he asked. 'I wonder sometimes . . .'

Fifteen minutes later, the Ghostbusters were fast asleep in their beds. A busy night chasing poltergeists had taken its toll and they slumbered heavily. Dreams soon transported them.

Egon Spengler dreamed of his latest and greatest invention. Winston dreamed of a ten-tier birthday cake made out of his favourite blueberry fudgecake. Ray dreamed of catching all the ghosts of New York in his trap. Peter dreamed of a good night's sleep with no alarm bells to wake him.

All four of them were lost to the world.

The storm raged on outside. Rain still fell in sheets. Thunder rolled and an occasional flash of lightning threw scary shadows on to the floor of the dormitory. It was not a night to be out and about. The Ghostbusters were in the best place.

'Weeeee.'

Slimer floated into the dormitory and hovered above the four beds. The Ghostbusters had been good friends. They had looked after him for a long time now. But he had let them down badly. It was time to go. He was not needed any more.

There was a wistful expression on his pallid face. He flew to Ray's bed and waved a last goodbye. Then he did the same beside Egon's bed. It was Winston's turn for a farewell next. Finally, Slimer came to Peter's bed.

He swallowed hard as he remembered.

The words came back to wound him again.

'He helps himself to everything that isn't nailed down or on fire!'

Slimer shuddered. There was truth in the accusation.

Peter was speaking for all the Ghostbusters.

They didn't like him any more.

Slimer was unable to raise his hand to wave goodbye. He lowered his head instead and floated away quietly to the hole in the floor. It was the last time he would see the Ghostbusters.

When he came into the reception area, the place was

empty. He went over to Janine's desk and took out a piece of paper. With a pencil in his hand, he scribbled a note then read through it.

Propping it up on the desk, he was ready to go. Then he noticed the party hat lying on the floor. He picked it up and put it on his head. The wistful smile again played on his face.

'Glug-glug-glug.'

He turned to go. Slimer flew straight through the wall but the hat could not go with him. Dislodged from his head, it fell in a crumpled heap to the floor. It was a sad memento of his final departure.

Rain was still pouring down as Slimer came out into the street. A few vehicles squished past but there were no pedestrians about to brave the foul weather. A blaze of lightning suddenly illumined the fire station with vivid effect.

Slimer had a last, sorrowful look at his old home.

'Weeeee!'

He was a small, sad, pathetic figure. He felt quite friendless in a hostile world. The fire station had been warm. Now he was out in the cold and the rain.

Slimer moved slowly away down the street.

It was time to find a new home.

Janine Melnitz was a tender-hearted young woman. She had seen how hurt Slimer had been when he was ticked off by Peter. Maybe the ghost *did* have feelings. She wanted to reassure him in some way. There was an obvious solution.

To give him food of some sort.

Janine went out to the all-night delicatessen. A raincoat and an umbrella kept out the worst of the downpour but she still got wet. Janine did not mind. Slimer came first.

In her hand she carried a large, full bag of groceries.

'Slimer!' she called. 'I'm back!'

She dumped the bag on the desk, parked her umbrella then slipped off her soaking raincoat. When she had hung it up to drip dry, she looked around for him.

'I brought you some doughnuts! C'mon Slimer!'

There was no reply. Janine was surprised. Mention of doughtnuts usually brought Slimer running. Any other time, he smelt fresh food as soon as she brought it in.

'Slimer!' she called. 'Where are you?'

Then she saw the note on her desk. She snatched it up.

'Oh no!'

She read through it and gasped in horror.

'Oh no, Slimer! No, no, no!'

Janine stuck out a fist and banged the alarm bell.

BRRING-BRRING! BRRING-BRRING! BRRING-BRRING!

From the top of the building came the sounds of panic and confusion as the Ghostbusters dragged themselves out of bed. They jumped into their overalls and came sliding down the pole.

Ray Stantz was the first to arrive. Wiping the sleep from his eyes, he staggered across to the secretary.

'What is it, Janine? Where's the problem?'

48

'Right here, Ray.'

Peter, Winston and Egon came sliding into view.

'Did we have another call?' asked Winston.

'No,' said Janine.

'It's not those poltergeists again?' said Egon.

'No,' she told him.

'I knew it,' said Peter, leaning over to Egon. 'Janine's gone over the edge. Too much coffee. I warned her.'

'Shhhh!' said Egon. 'She looks upset.'

'I am upset,' said Janine. 'This is an emergency.'

'Why?' said Peter.

'Slimer's run away from home!'

5

Seek Slimer

The Ghostbusters were flabbergasted. They reeled as if they had been struck by a blow. Ray was the first to recover.

'Would you repeat that, Janine?' he asked.

'Slimer's run away from home.'

'Are you *sure*?' said Winston.

'Absolutely certain.'

'But this is quite appalling!' said Egon with concern.

'He doesn't feel *wanted* here any more,' said Janine.

'Poor old Slimer!' sighed Ray.

Peter Venkman yawned and gave a dismissive gesture.

'If that's all it is, I'm going back to bed.'

'How can you do that?' said Janine. 'This is a crisis.'

'No, it isn't,' he replied confidently. 'Slimer wouldn't leave – he's got too good a deal going here.'

'Okay,' said Janine. 'Watch this.'

She held up the bag and crinkled the paper to make a noise.

'Doughnuts! Come and get 'em, Slimer!'

They waited for a few seconds. Nothing happened.

'That proves it,' decided Winston. 'He's gone.'

'He's not,' said Peter irritably. 'Slimer'd never go.'

'Oh no?' asked Janine. 'You don't think so?'

'I *know* so,' he insisted.

She picked up the note from her desk with a flourish.

'Listen to this,' she told them. ' "No-one likes me. I'm always doing bad things. I try, but I can't help it. So it's better if I leave. Goodbye forever. Slimer".'

Ray stepped right up to the desk and held out his hand.

'Can I see that, Janine?'

'Sure.'

She handed him the note. Ray found himself looking at a tangle of scrawls, doodles and squiggly lines. It was quite incomprehensible. He put the note down in front of her.

'You can read *this*?' he said in amazement.

'Of course,' she answered with great aplomb. 'I'm a secretary. I can read anything.'

'But it's a load of scribble,' contested Ray.

'He wrote it in a real hurry,' she explained. 'I guess he felt that the sooner he left, the happier someone here would be.'

They all turned to look at Peter with resentment.

There was clear hostility in their manner.

Peter was unperturbed. He held out his hands wide.

'Let me guess – this is all my fault, right?'

'Well, it sure ain't mine,' said Winston.

'Nor mine,' said Ray.

'Nor mine,' said Egon.

'Nor mine,' said Janine.

'That leaves me,' concluded Peter. 'I'm the villain.'

It was Winston who was the first to spring into action.

'It doesn't matter whose fault it was,' he said urgently. 'We've got to go after Slimer.'

'We're right behind you, Winston,' said Ray.

'We'll split up,' suggested Egon. 'That way we can cover the most area more quickly.'

They ran to the lockers and put on their equipment. Because it was raining outside, they all wore their Ghostbuster caps which had their logo imprinted on them.

Pausing at the door, they looked meaningfully at Peter.

'Best of luck, guys!' he said drily.

They went quickly out and slammed the door behind them.

Janine was disgusted at Peter's attitude.

'Aren't you going to look for him?'

'Who?'

'Slimer!'

'Me?' he said. 'You've gotta be joking. I'm the guy he slimed, remember? Go after *him*? Ha!'

He folded his arms and stood there with apparent resolution.

But he was as worried as the others inside.

Deep down, Peter was very fond of Slimer. But he was too proud to let it show. He continued to put on his act.

The rest of the Ghostbusters trudged along in the driving rain until they came to a major crossroads. They looked around in blank dismay.

'This is where we split up,' said Egon.

'He can't have gone very far,' said Winston hopefully. 'Let's hope we track him down.'

'Supposing we don't?' asked Egon mournfully.

'We *must*,' insisted Winston.

'Yeah, but supposing we don't?'

'Slimer's on the team,' reminded Ray. 'We need him.'

'We need to find him and *tell* him that,' said Winston. 'Slimer ought to realise that *we* want him even if Peter doesn't.'

'Peter has been a bit high-handed over this,' said Egon.

'He roughed Slimer up once too often,' said Ray.

'It's down to us now, guys,' observed Winston.

'Exactly,' said Egon solemnly. 'We must remember what Slimer is. A free-floating ghost. It's not safe for him to be loose in New York.'

'You mean — he might start *haunting* again?' said Ray.

'I mean that he might fall in with bad company,' explained Egon. 'We know him and love him as a benign spectre. But he could easily revert. We don't want him running with a pack of ghosts.'

'That would be terrible!' said Winston.

'Then let's find him,' urged Egon. 'Fast!'

They split up and went off down different streets.

It was one of their most important missions.

Finding Slimer was vital.

Unaware that he was being sought, Slimer made his way disconsolately along a deserted street. It was still very cold and damp and he was already missing the cosiness of the fire station. But there was no place for him there now and so he soldiered on.

'Weeee,' he moaned quietly to himself.

Suddenly, his eye kindled. He was cheered up at last.

'Guzz-guzz-guzz!'

Right in front of him was a shop window full of candy. He zipped over and stared through the glass. All his favourites were there. He licked his lips in anticipation. He would float through the window and help himself. It was easy.

Peter Venkman's voice held him back.

'He helps himself to anything that's not nailed down . . .'

Slimer pondered. He looked at the candy again and he was tempted. Floating through the window, he grabbed handfuls of it. But Peter's remark was like a distant echo in his ears.

'He helps himself to anything . . .'

Slimer's guilt stirred once more.

'Gurrr.'

He put the candy down and went back through the

window. He wanted to prove that he *could* behave properly when he put his mind to it. The candy was not his so he would leave it alone.

He floated aimlessly down the street until he came to a big store. Spotting his reflection in the window, he went over to examine it then he moved away. But there was a problem.

His reflection stayed right where he had left it.

He went to the window to take a second look. He smiled at his reflection but got no response. He waved at it but got no answering gesture. When he swivelled round so that he was floating upside down, the reflection remained where it was.

He was unsettled. It was ghostly.

Slimer pressed his nose against the window. His reflection swung its head to glare at him. It startled him.

'Oh!'

He moved quickly off and kept his eyes off the other windows. It was cruel. He was completely alone.

Even his own reflection had abandoned him.

Tears of distress began to run down his big face.

Janine Melnitz was seated behind her desk in the reception area back at Ghostbuster headquarters. Her head was buried in a magazine. There was no way that she could rest while Slimer was lost. She vowed to stay up all night until he was safely returned. Meanwhile, she was reading an absorbing article.

Peter Venkman tiptoed furtively down the stairs behind her. Convinced that Janine was lost in her reading,

he hoped to slip past her and go out through the door without her even knowing that he had been there. Peter got within a few paces of her. Taking a deep breath, he scuttled past.

Janine spoke without even looking up.

'Going somewhere!'

He let out a startled cry and clutched at his heart.

'Janine,' he begged, 'don't DO that!'

She regarded him cynically over the top of her glasses.

'I just thought that maybe you were going out to look for Slimer.'

Peter backed towards the door, gesturing defensively.

'Who – me?' he asked, trying to appear cool. 'Heck, no. I was just going out for a walk.'

'A walk?'

'Yeah – on my two legs.'

'In the rain?'

'Is it raining?' he asked, pretending to be surprised.

'Pouring. You'll be soaked.'

'Great!'

'You *want* to get wet?'

'Sure, why not?' he argued. 'New York rain's good for you. It has special properties. Doesn't harm you at all.' He gave her a little wave. 'Well, see you later.'

He crossed to the door and opened it.

'Just one thing,' she called after him.

'Yeah?' he replied, pausing for a moment.

Janine smiled for the first time in some while.

'If you should just *happen* to find Slimer . . .'

'Not a chance,' he said.

'If you should, Peter . . .'

'I won't,' he insisted.

'But if you do,' she continued easily. 'Tell him that-
. . . tell him that we miss him.'

It was Peter's turn to smile now.

He could not hide anything from Janine. She knew
him too well. He was as anxious as any of them to get
Slimer back and he was going out to help the others.
Janine understood that. It could remain unsaid between
them.

'Don't forget,' she reminded. 'Tell him to come home.'

'Will do,' said Peter.

He went out into the night to join in the search.

6

Slimer Makes Friends

The night grew steadily more miserable. There was heavier rain. The rumbles of thunder got deeper and the flashes of lightning became more spectacular. It seemed to be much colder.

Slimer floated despondently along a street. He was lost and alone. A taxi went past and sent up a small wave to soak him. It lowered his spirits even more. Tears welled up in his eyes again. It was no fun being out on his own on such a dreadful night.

He passed a row of houses. Light showed in a few windows. Everybody else was snug and warm in bed. They had homes. He did not. New York was an unkind place for an outcast like him. There was nowhere he could go.

He simply did not belong.

Weird noises then wafted through the air.

'Wheeeeeeeeeee!'

'Zaaaaaaaaaaaa!'

'Yahooooooooooo!'

It sounded as if somebody was having fun.

Slimer zipped on to the corner and looked around it. He was just in time to see a long, excitable stream of ghosts, ghouls and phantoms going up the steps of a tall, dark, dilapidated building. They were singing merrily as if going to some kind of party.

Slimer's hopes rose at once.

Parties meant food. Would he be invited?

'Guzz-guzz-guzz.'

He stopped to consider. The ghosts looked wild and ugly. He had lived with human beings for a long time now. Would they still accept him in the spirit world? Did he really want to go back? Would he be betraying his old friends if he did so?

Slimer looked up at the building. It reached high into the sky and bright beams shone out from windows on different floors. Some very powerful supernatural force was inside.

Lightning flashed to silhouette the building.

It was at once menacing and welcoming.

Slimer was in two minds about what he should do.

Had he come home?

'Guzz-guzz-guzz.'

He floated hesitantly towards the entrance.

Peter Venkman was having no luck in his search. With the heavy Proton Pack on his back, he walked through the wet streets and yelled at the top of his voice.

'Slimer! Slimer, where are you?'

His cries seemed to echo for miles through the city.

'Come home, Slimer! All is forgiven!'

Peter had second thoughts.

'Well – most of it, anyway.'

He and Slimer had fallen out from time to time but Peter put all that behind him now. He missed his little friend. And he was worried about him being out alone at night.

'Slimer!' he called in desperation. 'We *want* you!'

But Slimer did not hear him. He was mesmerised by the bright light coming from inside the building. Going up the steps, he went into the entrance hall and came to a halt. Inside was a succession of galleries stretching right on up to the roof. The size of the place was intimidating.

Yet there was no sign of anybody. It felt empty.

'Creeeeeeeeak!'

Double doors inched open with a squeak on the other side of the hall. Light and noise filtered out. Slimer went slowly towards the doors and peeped in through the gap between them.

'Yaheeeeee!'

'Zuk-zuk-zuk-zuk-zuk!'

'Whoooooooo!'

'Ticky-ticky-ticky-ticky-ticky!'

At a long table, the ghosts and ghouls seemed to have gathered for some kind of banquet. They laughed and chatted away. There was a sense of companionship that appealed to Slimer. The demons were hideous, the

monsters were deformed and the apparitions were grotesque but that did not matter.

They were part of an exclusive brotherhood.

And they were happy to be together.

Slimer watched them with gathering interest.

'Guzz-guzz-guzz!'

The noise subsided and they all looked towards the doors. For a moment, Slimer was alarmed but his fears were groundless. They did not see him as an intruder at all. They began to wave him across to join them.

A slow smile spread across his face. The huge teeth came into view. There were answering smiles all around. It gave him a tremendous thrill. They wanted him to join them.

Slimer had come in out of the cold at last.

He was one of them.

As he floated across the room, they made room for him on one of the benches. He sat down between a dragon-like monster and a one-eyed phantom. The whole assembly gave him a welcome.

'Hooray! Hooray!'

There was a spontaneous round of applause.

'Glug-glug-glug!' said Slimer gratefully.

He was soon caught up in the mad chatter of his new friends.

A gigantic shadow appeared on the wall behind him then materialised into the pig-faced creature with the black cloak and top hat. Gazing down at the ghostly get-together, he looked like some kind of weird magician.

He bared his pointed teeth as he gave a long cackle.

'Yahaaaaaaaaaaaaaaaaaaaa!'

A new member had joined them.

Slimer did not realise that there would be a price to pay.

After a long and fruitless search, Ray, Egon and Winston met up again at a corner. They compared notes.

'You two find anything?' asked Ray.

'Nope,' admitted Winston.

'Not a thing,' said Egon.

'Same here,' confessed Ray.

Egon held out his PKE meter and it began to flash. Both of its wings were vibrating and it was clearly picking up some signals. Ray indicated the meter.

'Something up, Egon?' he asked.

'Very definitely,' replied the other.

'What is it?'

'Gentlemen,' said Egon, 'we have a scientific dilemma.'

'A *what*?' gulped Winston.

Egon peered at his meter and scratched his head.

'It's baffling,' he said. 'I was just thinking about those poltergeists we fought earlier on. We shouldn't have lost that battle.'

'But we did,' recalled Winston ruefully.

'They were too strong for us,' added Ray.

'That's where the dilemma comes in,' explained Egon. 'They *shouldn't* have been so strong.

Poltergeists are supposed to get weaker the farther they are from home.'

Ray thought about it for a second then snapped his fingers.

'Unless they were drawing on some other source of energy.'

'Yeah,' agreed Winston. 'And since ghosts are almost pure energy, every time a new member joins them, their power increases. They become more dangerous.'

Egon looked more solemn and worried than ever.

'Exactly,' he said. 'It's like hooking more and more batteries to the same line. You increase the voltage all the time.'

'That's what the poltergeists must be doing,' decided Ray.

'I'm afraid so,' said Egon. 'With that sort of power, they could go anywhere they want. If I'm right, then even one more ghost could make all the difference.'

Winston and Ray traded a look of alarm.

'*Slimer*?' they said in unison.

'Slimer,' confirmed Egon.

'Not him,' claimed Ray.

'No,' said Winston. 'He's such a sweet little guy.'

'At the moment,' Egon pointed out. 'But not if he joined those poltergeists.'

'He wouldn't do that,' asserted Ray.

'Slimer might not have the choice,' said Egon.

'That's terrible!' exclaimed Winston.

'It's terrifying,' warned Egon. 'If they stole his energy, they could become almost unbeatable. And immensely evil and wicked. They could become the most powerful force in the whole country. With the addition of one more ghost.'

'Slimer?' they muttered.

'Even Slimer.'

It was a grim thought. New urgency was injected.

'We'd better find Slimer before those poltergeists do,' said Winston with an edge of desperation.

'Let's split up,' advised Ray.

'Search *everywhere*!' pressed Egon. 'If we don't find him soon, he'll become part of their malignant power as it sweeps across America. Slimer may be innocent enough in himself. But he could be the difference between victory and defeat for those poltergeists. He must be stopped!'

They raced off in opposite directions.

Peter Venkman seemed to have walked down half the streets of the city in search of Slimer but it had all been in vain. Every time he called out his friend's name, he heard what he thought were echoes in the far distance. When he listened more carefully, he realised that the cries were coming from the other Ghostbusters.

'Slimerrrrr!' yelled Peter, cupping his hands to form a megaphone. 'Slimerrrrrr!'

'Slimerrrrr!' shouted Winston under a dark bridge some three blocks away. 'Slimerrrrr!'

'Slimerrrrr!' boomed Egon into an apartment block in the downtown area. 'Slimerrrrr!'

'Slimerrrrr!' called Ray into a big hall. 'Slimerrrrr!'

Everybody else in New York could hear the name.
Why couldn't Slimer himself?

Peter tried once more. He stood in the middle of a deserted street and filled his lungs. Then he gave his most full-throated bellow yet.

'SLIMERRRRRR!'

His cry had an immediate effect.

A taxi came haring towards him.

Back in the dilapidated building, Slimer was enjoying a talk with his new companions. They giggled joyfully as they discussed their favourite hauntings and talked of the mischief they had been able to create. Slimer laughed along with the rest of them.

A monstrous shadow then fell across the entire table.

The pig-faced creature loomed high above them.

He pointed a long, sinewy finger directly at Slimer.

The little ghost bounced up and down with embarrassment.

'Glug-glug-glug . . . *Me*?'

The creature nodded then beckoned him forward.

Quaking with fear, Slimer hovered in mid-air. He soon understood what he had to do. As a newcomer, he had to go through a kind of audition. The creature wanted to see just how ghostlike a ghost he could be.

Slimer responded willingly.

Screwing up his features, he pulled his ugliest face and made a disgusting sound with his tongue. Then he gnashed his teeth wildly and emitted a low groan.

The creature was not impressed in the least.

His long finger invited Slimer to follow.

'Oh-oh!' said the little ghost, sensing real trouble.

With a mad cackle, the pig-faced creature wrapped his cloak around him then flew straight out through the wall. He was taking Slimer out to show him something.

The ghost had no option.

He had to follow his new master.

7

The Search is On

Egon Spengler let his PKE meter dictate his footsteps for him. Staring at its dial, he walked down endless streets and did not even notice that he had entered a very run-down neighbourhood. Lights were few and far between. Danger lurked in the shadows.

Eyes fixed firmly on his meter, he went on regardless.

A group of punks were lounging in a doorway.

They saw him coming and stiffened at once.

'Okay, guys,' said their leader. 'We're in luck.'

'Let *me* take him,' grunted an ape-like youth with massive shoulders and over-long arms. 'I like mugging mugs.'

'It's *my* turn,' snarled a youth with a Mohican haircut.

'Leave him to *me*!' ordered the leader.

Unconscious of the peril that lay ahead, Egon strolled calmly on. When he walked past the group, he found that he had a companion. The youth was tall, brawny

and wearing dark glasses. His crew-cut gave him the appearance of a convict.

The leader of the punks went into his usual patter.

'Well, well,' he said. 'What's wrong man? You lose something?'

'Yes, actually,' murmured Egon.

'Hey, maybe we can help you find it.'

'Thank you.'

'What'd it look like?'

Egon's face was as expressionless as usual. Still watching his PKE meter, he spoke in a flat, unemotional voice.

'I'm looking for a full torso ectoplasmic manifestation, colour green, no legs, spirit classification unknown.'

The leader of the punks stopped in his tracks.

'Oh, yeah . . . er, good luck!'

Egon walked out of a danger he had not even recognised.

The rest of the gang converged on their leader.

'What happened?' demanded the ape.

'We had him!' growled the Mohican haircut.

'Why'd you let him go?' asked the ape.

The leader gazed after the departing figure of Egon.

'My dad always told me — "Never mess with anybody weirder than you are!"'

The punks nodded sagely. It was sound advice.

Slimer followed his new master through the dark streets on an expedition. He was to be given a lesson in haunting. The pig-like creature stopped beside a chimney when he saw two young men walking together along the street. It was the perfect opportunity.

He turned to Slimer and hissed a command.

'Watch this!'

'Glug-glug-glug!'

'Now!'

Inflating himself to his full size, the creature swooped down on the two young men with predatory zeal. His mouth was open, his fangs bared and his eyes blazing. A blood-curdling yell rang out from his throat.

'Eeyaaaaaaaaaaaaaaa!!!!'

The young men almost jumped out of their skins.

'Oh my Gawd!'

'Run!'

They turned tail and stampeded off at full speed.

The pig-faced ghost had put the fear of death into them and he celebrated with a malicious cackle. Then he turned back to Slimer who had watched it all without enthusiasm.

'See?' asked the monster.

'Glug-glug.'

'Now — *you*.'

'Oo!' said Slimer diffidently.

He did not enjoy frightening human beings. Slimer was by nature a friendly spirit. But he had no choice in the matter. His new master gave the commands.

They went off in search of fresh prey.

Egon Spengler kept walking until he came to a square with a fountain at the centre of it. Water cascaded down

from the spout at the top and the rain swelled the flow. Leaning against the fountain as if relaxing in a deck chair was Ray Stantz.

Astonished to see him there, Egon went over to him.

'Why aren't you looking for Slimer?' he asked.

'I am,' said Ray.

'Here?'

'It's a new theory of mine.'

'Theory?'

'Yeah,' explained Ray. 'Ever notice how, if you go looking for someone, you almost never find them?'

'So?'

'Well, I figure if I wait in one place, everybody I met in my entire life will come by sooner or later.'

'Including Slimer?'

'Especially Slimer.' Ray grinned broadly. 'Get me, Egon. I go looking for him by staying right here.'

Egon gave him a shrewd glance. He wondered if his friend had cracked up in some way. He spoke very gently to him.

'Ray, I think you should know that that's the most absurd and ridiculous theory I've heard in my —'

He broke off abruptly as a car came to a halt nearby.

'Ray Stanz!' called a woman's voice. 'Hi!'

A grandmotherly lady was hailing him from the car.

'That's Mrs Millikan, my second-grade teacher.' He waved back to her. 'Hi!'

The car drove off into the darkness.

'I told you,' said Ray. 'They all come by.'

Egon shook his head in utter disbelief.

'Ray,' he confided. 'I think one of us needs a long, long vacation.'

Egon wondered if *he* was mad and not his colleague.

The pig-faced monster zoomed across the rooftops with Slimer in tow. When he saw a lone figure coming along a sidewalk, he hovered in mid-air and pointed a bony finger downwards.

Slimer hesitated and shook his head.

'Er-ah-nooooo!'

'Yes!' ordered the other.

'Gurrrrr . . . *Me*?'

'Go get him!'

'Ooooo!'

'Now!' roared the monster.

Slimer flew down to the adjacent street and lurked near the corner. He waited as he heard footsteps approach then gathered up all his strength and venom to scare the hapless pedestrian.

Slimer did not know who was around the corner.

It was Peter Venkman, still searching for his friend.

He looked into doorways, he lifted the lids of trash cans, he peered under parked vehicles. Eager to find Slimer, he even peeped through letterboxes.

'Now, if I were Slimer,' he said, 'what would I do?'

He searched a litter bin attached to a post.

It was empty.

'Poor guy!' sighed Peter. 'I'm almost ready to forgive him for all the times he slimed me.' He considered this offer. *'Almost,'* he stressed.

79

He was now almost at the corner and he had no idea of the ambush that had been set up. His heart was heavy.

'Boy! Would I love to see his ugly face come round that corner!' he said affectionately.

Peter got his wish sooner than he expected.

Gearing himself up, Slimer zipped around the corner.

'Arrrrrrrrrrrrrr!' he growled.

'Slimer!' said Peter with delight. 'There you are.'

'Oooo!'

Slimer wanted to stop but it was too late. He was on a collision course. As Peter grinned a welcome at him, he went straight into his old friend and knocked him flat.

'Splattttttt!'

Peter was covered in slime from waist to head.

'Oh no!' he moaned.

Slimer shot back around the corner. He was very distressed. Peter was the last person he wanted to attack. He now felt more guilty than ever. The Ghostbusters would never want him back after this. Slimer had ruined everything.

He sobbed quietly then a huge shadow enveloped him.

It was his new master.

Slimer had to follow him.

Peter, meanwhile, was looking skyward in astonishment.

'I don't believe it!' he wailed. 'He did it to me again.'

Taking the walkie-talkie set from his belt, he extended

the aerial then spoke into the microphone. His voice had a false brightness in it.

'Hello, fellas,' he said. 'Guess what? I found Slimer. Peter – out!'

He let his head fall back against the ground.

Back at the derelict building, the ghostly gathering had swelled in size. Fresh phantoms and new apparitions kept floating in every minute. It was like a convention of all the spirits in the city of New York. The banqueting hall was filling up.

Slimer returned to the place reluctantly. He no longer felt at ease there. His new master was not at all like the affable Ghostbusters. Slimer was forced to do evil things.

The pig-faced monster flew to the head of the table and drew himself up to his full height. He was a towering figure of evil. His cackle of pleasure was chilling.

'Welcome!' he hissed. 'Welcome, my friends!'

The ghosts bounced happily up and down in their seats.

'Whooo!'

'Yaheeee!'

'Chuk-chuk-chuk!'

The monster's voice was a loud, persuasive hiss.

'I am Ghash!' he said. 'Your master!'

Slimer began to tremble. He knew that something ghastly was in the offing. He tried to look away but Ghash held his gaze like a hypnotist.

'Now,' whispered Ghash.

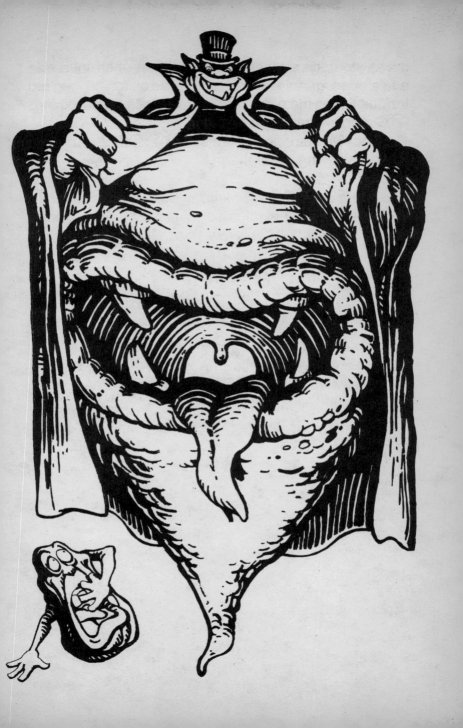

His stomach suddenly inflated to an enormous size and a huge, grinning mouth appeared on it. The long red tongue licked the giant lips. The stomach was drooling.

'Come!' invited Ghash.

Slimer was petrified.

He was going to eat them!

8

Slimer à la Carte

Peter Venkman had cleaned off the worst of the slime by the time the others got to him. A few blobs lingered on his shoulders and on his chest. The memory of the sliming stayed fresh in his mind. Nothing could wipe that away.

The other Ghostbusters were delighted to see him.

'Hi, Peter!' said Winston.

'We knew you'd join in the search party,' said Egon.

'Yeah,' added Ray. 'You're as keen as any of us to get Slimer back again.'

'Who is?' growled Peter.

'You are,' returned Winston. 'So stop pretending.'

'Why should *I* want him back?' asked Peter with outstretched palms. 'All he ever does to me is to slime me!'

'Come off it, Peter,' said Egon.

'You couldn't wait to look for him,' argued Ray.

'I was taking a walk, that's all,' said Peter.

'Oh sure,' mocked Winston.

'I was.'

'And I suppose you just happened to bump into Slimer?' teased Winston.

'Yes! I mean – no!'

'Make up your mind,' advised Egon.

'It was Slimer who bumped into me!' complained Peter.

'By accident?' asked Ray.

'No! He took a deliberate run at me!' Peter was still angry. 'I should've busted him ages ago!'

'That's an awful thing to say!' chided Winston.

'Well, I'm fed up with him!'

'Yeah,' said Winston. 'You made that clear back at the station. But for you, we wouldn't be out here now.'

Ray looked very carefully at Peter.

'You're *sure* you saw Slimer?' he asked.

Peter indicated the blobs on his chest.

'How else do you think *this* happened?'

'Don't kid me,' said Ray. 'I've seen you eat.'

Winston burst out laughing. Peter fumed.

Egon was consulting his PKE meter. It was flashing madly and its antennae were quivering frantically. He took a reading and his eyebrows raised in concern.

'This doesn't look good, guys.'

'Neither does this slime on me,' said Peter.

'Back off, Peter,' advised Ray. 'This is serious.'

'Deadly serious,' agreed Egon.

'What's happened?' said Winston.

'It's started.'

'What has?' asked Peter.

'Remember those poltergeists?' said Egon.

'Will I ever forget them!'

'We think Slimer's joined them, Peter.'

'Never!'

'He has,' insisted Egon. 'Against his will, probably. But then he has nobody else he can turn to, I guess. They seemed like friends at first. He was suckered in.'

'What will happen to him?' said Peter with anxiety.

'He could be swallowed up,' explained Egon.

'Our little Slimer!'

'He's a ghost, Peter,' reminded Egon. 'That makes him a vital source of energy.'

'We must get to him right away!' urged Winston.

'How close is he?' asked Ray.

'Very close indeed – according to the meter.'

Egon led them down a street and around a corner.

'There it is, guys!' he declared.

'Woweeee!'

'Will you look at that!'

'Amazing!'

Facing them was the tall, bizarre structure where the ghosts were all assembling. Beams of light shot out from windows on every floor and deep chords of music could be heard. An odd smell was coming from the building and it was positively throbbing with spectral energy.

'I guess we found it okay,' said Egon lugubriously.

His meter flashed, crackled and bleeped all at once.

'Give us a reading,' said Winston.

Egon watched the needle flickering wildly on its dial.

'The individual frequencies are merging,' he announced. 'All the small ghosts in there are being merged into one big ectoplasmic mass. If this goes on, it will become all-powerful.'

'And Slimer?' asked Peter.

'Supposing *he's* in there?' said Winston.

'And supposing he's already been absorbed?' said Ray.

Egon shook his head. His face was quite funereal.

'Then we may never be able to separate him.'

'He'll be gone for good!' gasped Ray.

'I'm afraid so.'

Peter shrugged and introduced a flippant note.

'That means we'll have to zap, trap and contain them all – including Slimer.' He gave them a cheerful grin. 'Kind of makes it a perfect day, doesn't it?'

They glared at him with quiet fury.

He waved his hands at them in a calming gesture.

'Just a joke, fellas,' he soothed. 'Lighten up.'

'Slimer's in there,' reminded Winston.

'He needs us,' said Ray.

'So?' replied Peter. 'Let's go get him.'

The Ghostbusters headed purposefully for the building.

A titanic struggle lay ahead.

But they had to rescue Slimer somehow.

The whole place was now buzzing with activity. Ghosts were drifting up through the air to Ghash in a never-ending stream. The hideous pig-face had disappeared from his stomach but it was still vast. As the ghosts went in through the stomach walls, it got even bigger. It almost filled the room.

Ghash was getting more and more powerful.

'Oooooo!'

Slimer was highly disturbed by it all.

When a ghost grabbed his hand and dragged him towards the monster, he quickly shook himself free. He did not want to be merged with the others. Slimer liked his independent existence.

If he could possibly hold on to it.

Looking for an escape, he flew across to the double doors but a new influx of ghosts came through them and he was caught up in them. They sailed upwards to go through into the now enormous stomach of the cackling Ghash. What surprised Slimer was that they all seemed so happy to surrender their separate identities.

'Te-hee-te-hee-te-hee-te-hee!'

'Yum-yum-yum-yum-yum-yum-yum!'

'Zik-zik-zik-zik-zik!'

At the last moment, Slimer managed to flit away.

He went for the doors again but more ghosts poured in. He had to fight his way clear. They might want to give in but he did not. Slimer put a hand on the door handle but got no further.

A hiss like a whirlwind surged around the room.

'You!'

Slimer spun around with his teeth chattering.

'M-m-m-me?'

'Come!' beckoned Ghash.

'Gurr . . .'

'Come!'

The monster's index finger curled inwards as he invited Slimer to him. Though the little ghost tried to resist, he could not. A strong and irresistible force drew him upwards like a magnet.

'Ooo-ah-ooo!'

His protests were in vain.

Slimer was absorbed through the stomach walls.

He had been swallowed up at last.

The Ghostbusters stood in the entrance hall and looked up at the ascending galleries. There was not a soul in sight and yet the weird light and music was building to a crescendo.

'Where is everybody?' asked Winston.

'They'll be here soon enough,' warned Egon.

'Slimer!' yelled Ray. 'We've come to take you home.'

There was no answer. Peter took over.

'Slimer! Come on out and slime me again!'

There was still no reply.

'As I feared,' said Egon. 'We arrived too late.'

'Those ghosts must be *somewhere*!' insisted Winston.

They were. Inside Ghash's monstrous stomach.

'WHOOOOOOOOOSH!'

A fierce wind blew the double doors open and a long cloud of smoke came out. It spiralled upwards and then took on the daunting form of Ghash. The pig-faced

creature now possessed immense energy and he gloried in it.

'Ya-haaaaaaaaaaaaaaaa!'

His cackle made them put their hands to their ears.

Although the ghosts were all in his stomach, they had not yet been assimilated properly. They could still be seen moving around and pushing at the stomach walls. As the Ghostbusters stared up at the grisly sight, they recognised the outline of someone they knew and loved.

Slimer was trying to get back out again.

'There he is!' said Ray, pointing.

'He hasn't been absorbed properly yet,' noted Winston.

'Any hope of getting him outta there?' asked Peter.

'I can barely read his frequency,' said Egon, staring at his meter. 'He's getting weak. We're losing him.'

'We mustn't give up!' urged Winston.

'He's our pal!' said Ray.

Egon thought for a second then reached a decision.

'Just one chance,' he concluded. 'Set your proton beams at five hundred thousand megahertz – Slimer's frequency.'

They made the adjustments to their particle throwers.

'I hope you know what you're doing, Egon,' said Peter.

'So do I,' he admitted.

Their guns were now fully charged.

'Ready,' said Winston.

'Ready,' said Ray.

'Ready,' said Peter.
'Then here goes!' said Egon. 'Stand by!'
It was their last possible hope.
Slimer's struggles were getting weaker.
It was now or never.

9

Guzz-guzz-guzz

The four Ghostbusters aimed their guns at the tiny figure of Slimer, which was clearly visible as it clutched at the stomach wall of the monster. Their technology might save him yet.

Egon gave the command to fire.

'Now!'

Particle beams shot out simultaneously from the weapons.

'KERWHAMM!'

Their concentrated power was right on target.

'Don't worry, Slimer!' shouted Ray.

'We'll have you out in a second!' promised Winston.

'Okay?' said Egon. 'All together – pull!'

Gripping their Proton Guns tightly, the Ghostbusters lifted them up so that they snapped with a whiplash effect. Slimer was yanked hard towards them.

Ghash's stomach was like an enormous piece of elastic. It bent and bent as they tugged to pull Slimer free. Finally, he came right through and out into the air again.

'Pop!'

'Hooray!' they cheered.

But Slimer still had problems.

Pulled out with such force, he was now thrown around the entrance hall like a squash ball and he bounced from wall to wall for several seconds. When he finally landed on the ground, he was dizzy. But he was also profoundly grateful to his friends.

'Glug-glug-glug!'

'Don't mention it, Slimer,' said Winston.

'Great to have you back!' called Ray.

'We still have unfinished business,' noted Egon.

They turned back to the towering form of Ghash.

'Yeah,' said Peter. 'Now for Mr Ugly himself . . .'

They recharged their guns but got no chance to use them.

'Wheeesh!'

Their weapons and their Proton Packs were whisked away and sent spinning in the air. Ghash glared down at them with wicked satisfaction. They were now completely unarmed.

Ray Stantz spoke to Peter in a hoarse whisper.

'That's what happens when you call him names.'

'All I said was Mr –' began Peter.

But Ray clapped a hand over his mouth to stop him.

'I think we're in a LOT of trouble here,' said Winston.

'Yes,' agreed Egon, looking up at the giant creature. 'He has almost unlimited power at his control.'

Peter had got free of Ray's hand now.

'It doesn't make him any less ugly,' he observed.

Ghash's eyes glowed like bonfires, then lightning bolts came flashing out of them and all but hit the Ghostbusters. They jumped out of the way as flames licked at them.

'He's getting a bit over-heated,' said Winston.

'You don't suppose that thing would listen to reason, do you?' asked Peter.

'Doubtful,' said Ray. 'Very doubtful.'

More lightning bolts shot down at them and they had to take evasive action. Small fires started all around them. Ghash was obviously determined to get them somehow.

'He looks real mean!' said Egon with concern.

'How do we fight a thing *that* size?' asked Winston.

'He's got the combined energy of all those ghosts,' said Ray.

'Minus one,' added Peter, nodding across to Slimer.

Ghash's eyes glowed again and he aimed them at the wooden floorboards directly in front of the Ghostbusters.

'FLASH!'

Four shafts of lightning came down this time and burned their way into the knotted wood. There was an immediate effect.

'TWANG!'

Long strips of wood curled up from the floor and wrapped themselves around the Ghostbusters. All four of them were held fast. It took their breath away.

'Hey! Let go!'

'Watch it!'

'Let's not get personal here, okay!'

'Put me down!'

Ghash emitted a frightening cackle of triumph.

Then he motioned with his finger and the coiled wood began to move upward. The Ghostbusters were slowly raised towards the gaping mouth of the monster. His razor-sharp teeth glistened and his red tongue hung out.

He was hungry. They would be his next meal.

The Ghostbusters protested for all their worth.

'Leave me alone. I taste horrible!'

'Meat-eating is bad for you!'

'Become a vegetarian!'

'Leave us alone. You don't know where we've been!'

But they were taken ever nearer the cavernous mouth.

'Oh boy!' howled Winston.

'Egon,' said Peter. 'I want you to know that this isn't my idea of a night on the town!'

'I agree,' replied Egon. 'This is one scientific experience that I'd be happy to miss out on.'

'I've got only one comment to make,' said Ray.

They all made it with him and yelled in unison.

'HELP!!!!'

Slimer got up from the floor and shook himself. His friends had saved him but they had put their own lives in danger. He had to rescue them somehow.

Their Proton Packs and guns lay on the floor. Slimer dived for them and grabbed the nearest gun. Having no idea how it worked, he pressed the only button he could see.

'SHEZAMM!'

A particle beam shot out at random and sliced through the strands of wood that held the Ghostbusters. Within chomping distance of the huge mouth, they were snatched away and fell to the floor.

'SHEZAMM!'

The gun went off again and its beam hit Ghash in the leg. He howled with rage and hopped on one foot. Slimer had proved something. The creature could be hurt.

'Grab your guns, fellas!' ordered Peter.

They obeyed the command at once and levelled their weapons up at Ghash. His eyes smouldered once more but he was not the only one with firepower now. Ghostbusters could hit back.

'Let's give him the works!' urged Winston.

'Full blast!' advised Egon.

'All together now!' shouted Ray.

'If you're that hungry, fella!' taunted Peter. 'Eat some Protons . . . Fire!'

They cut loose with their particle beams.

'ZAAAAAAAAP!'

'Arghhhhhhhh!' roared Ghash.

The monster was surrounded in a field of flashing energy. He fought hard to get away and the ghosts inside him put up their own battles. But the Ghostbusters had a firm hold on them all.

'Bring 'em down real slow!' said Peter.

'Come on, guys,' invited Winston as they drew the creature down. 'We got just the place for you.'

'Yeah,' said Ray. 'Warm and cosy inside.'

'Got the trap ready, Egon?' said Peter.

'Check.'

Egon pressed the switch and the ghost-trap flapped open. As the monster got closer to it, the trap exerted a tremendous suction power and pulled him down. The huge figure of Ghash got smaller and smaller. Along with all the other ghosts who had been absorbed into him, he was sucked straight into the trap.

'Clang!'

Its steel jaws snapped shut.

Steam began to rise from it and it vibrated insistently.

'Oh no!' said Egon.

'What's the trouble?' asked Peter.

'I'm not sure the trap can hold all those ghosts at one time,' explained Egon. 'It might be overloaded.'

Ray picked it up and examined it closely.

'The trap won't hold that lot indefinitely.'

'Right,' announced Winston. 'I think we'd better get this thing contained – pronto – before it blows!'

'What an awfully good idea, Winston,' said Peter, then he turned to Slimer. 'Oh, and I guess *you* can come, too.'

Slimer's grin took up half his face.

'Glug-glug-glug!'

Ecto-I rocketed back to the fire station and skidded to a halt. The trap was ticking away like a time bomb and

they knew that it could explode at any moment. Winston raced down to the basement with it and Slimer followed him. The others stayed in the reception area with Janine.

'No time to waste!' said Winston to himself.

He pulled down the metal drawer in the middle of the containment system and the green light changed to red. Inserting the trap, he pulled a handle. The contents of the trap were then jettisoned into the unit. The introduction of so much spectral energy made the whole system gurgle and vibrate.

'You can do it, baby!' encouraged Winston.

The containment unit was equal to the task. The shuddering stopped and the green light came on again. The danger was over. Ghash and the other ghosts were now well and truly contained.

'See?' said Winston. 'A piece of cake.'

Mention of food whetted Slimer's appetite.

'Guzz-guzz-guzz!'

'Talking of which . . .' continued Winston.

He took Slimer up the stairs to the reception area. It was almost dark in there. They moved towards the desk and the lights snapped on to reveal that the room was festooned with party decorations once more.

'Surprise!' they chorused. 'Welcome home, Slimer!'

'Glug-glug-glug!' he squealed in delight.

'This is just our way of saying we missed you,' explained Ray. 'But don't you *ever* do that again.'

'The party was Peter's idea,' said Janine.

Slimer was touched. He went across to Peter and

purred at him. For once, Peter was a little embarrassed.

'Give me a break, okay?' he said. 'So I like parties. It's got nothing to do with slime-skin here.' He tried to sound casual as he addressed Slimer. 'And I didn't miss you.'

Slimer looked devastated. Peter gave a half-smile.

'Well, maybe just a little.'

Slimer glowed. They were friends again.

The real treat was yet to come. Winston went over to the filing cabinets and wheeled out a trolley from behind them. On it was a large cardboard box. On top of that was a huge birthday cake with marzipan and icing.

'Enough talking!' said Winston. 'We got two parties to make up for, you know.'

But Slimer had eyes only for the cake. His self-control vanished once again and he revved himself up to pounce. Zipping across the room, he opened his mouth and took the whole cake in one greedy bite.

When he realised what he had done, he was *very* ashamed.

The Ghostbusters were very understanding.

'Don't worry, Slimer,' said Egon.

He lifted the box to reveal a second cake on the trolley.

'Yeah,' said Peter. 'Even scientists learn from their mistakes. One for you, one for us. Now, let's eat!'

'Hey,' said Ray, jerking a thumb towards Slimer. 'Speaking of learning, I taught Slimer a new trick.'

The others turned to the little ghost with interest.

'All right, Slimer,' said Ray with mischievous glee. 'Go ahead – show them your food.'

Slimer grinned and made dreadful gurgling sounds.
Then the cake began to reappear.
'Stop it!' yelled Peter.
'That's disgusting!' scolded Janine.
'I can't bear to watch!' howled Egon.
'Who wants to eat *now*?' wailed Winston.
The party trick stopped the party.
Slimer had come home.

If you have enjoyed SLIMER, COME HOME, you might like to read the other *Real Ghostbuster* titles from Knight Books:

THE REAL GHOSTBUSTERS No. 1

JANINE'S GENIE

by Kenneth Harper

When a client offers the Ghostbusters the pick of his belongings instead of payment, Janine chooses a ridiculous, old brass oil-lamp and unleashes a load of trouble on to town, in the shape of a lampful of ghosts and ghouls.

KNIGHT BOOKS

THE REAL GHOSTBUSTERS No. 2

GHOSTS-R-US

by Kenneth Harper

When Slimer unwittingly releases a par-
ticularly unpleasant family of ghosts, the
Ghostbusters team find themselves with
competition on their hands of a ghastly
ghostly kind.

KNIGHT BOOKS

GHOSTBUSTERS ™

novelisation by Larry Milne

(based on the screenplay by
Dan Aykroyd and Harold Ramis)

Who or what can deliver New York from the
dreaded tyranny of the paranormal? Who can
save the city from a plague of ghosts that will
spare no living creature and leave no street
unvisited?

Who but a half crazed trio called the Ghostbusters. Poised between genius and lunacy,
these cosmic crusaders alone have the power
to combat a force unknown to human kind . . .

CORONET

MASK

MOBILE ARMOURED STRIKE KOMMAND

novelisation by Kenneth Harper

Imagine a world where there is more to reality than meets the eye. Where illusion and deception team up with man and machine to create a world of sophisticated vehicles and weaponry, manned by agents and counter agents. Look out for:–

VENICE MENACE
The MASK mission: to thwart VENOM's evil plans in one of the world's most beautiful cities, with the assistance of Scott Trakker and his courageous robot companion T-Bob.

BOOK OF POWER
The revered Book of Power, holder of mystical and ancient secrets, is sought by VENOM's leader, Miles Mayhem, whose wicked intention is to turn its magic to his own ends. The MASK mission is to return the book intact to its rightful guardians, but faced with VENOM's evil, the task is not easy.

KNIGHT BOOKS

PANDA POWER
When all the Chinese pandas are stolen from the nature preserves, MASK is not long in finding out who lies behind the crime. Why a celebrated sculptor should be kidnapped as well though, is more puzzling and increases the alarm.

THE PLUNDER OF GLOW-WORM GROTTO
Venom's leader, Miles Mayhem has hatched a chilling plot to steal the sacred pearls, the precious Maori heirlooms, from their secret grotto. Scott Trakker and his robot companion T-Bob help MASK in a perilous situation.

KNIGHT BOOKS